Teacher, Why Can't You Hear Me Raising My Hand?

Teacher, Why Can't You Hear Me Raising My Hand?

10 Strategies for Building Positive Teacher-Student Relationships

LLOYD W. SIZEMORE

Independent Publishing
Kindle Direct Publishing

Edited by Ariss Raybourn
Foreword by Allison Bowsman
Preface by Cheri B. Sizemore, Ed.D.
Photo by Alexa Tucker, The Jaxlo Agency

Manufactured in the United States of America.
ISBN: 9798553552145

The Teacher & The Poet

When I was a student and would read the words of Homer and Shakespeare, I was always amazed that I was taking in the thoughts and lessons from hundreds to thousands of years in the past.

Recently a former student contacted me to let me know that he was teaching his son a method of organizing information that he had learned in my class.

As I thought about the fact that he was passing on knowledge to his child that I had passed on from my teachers, it occurred to me that someday his child might pass on this knowledge to his own child and that I would have impacted the lives of children that I will never meet.

Poets, by their words, guarantee their own form of immortality by creating written thoughts that impact our souls.

I believe that teachers are like poets. Each day in the classrooms, they create their own unique forms of immortality.

Lloyd Sizemore

TABLE OF CONTENTS

Teacher, Why Can't You Hear Me Raising My Hand?

DEDICATION

To my wife, Cheri, for encouragement and input

To my children, Melanie, Matthew, Michael and
Mason and their spouses,
Josh, Chanel, Nicole and Lexy
Who have been willing to share the stories of their
own educational experiences

To my grandchildren, Evie and Tucker Sizemore,
Campbell and Harper Radde
I hope you are inspired by your future teachers

To the thousands of students who sat in my
classrooms
Thank you for sharing your stories

To Tommy Hayes and JoAnn Kelley, principals who
gave me permission to teach the way I wanted,
tolerated my independent thinking and listened to my
opinions on what I thought was best for the students.

FOREWORD

Twenty years ago I entered Mr. Sizemore's class knowing that history was not my favorite subject. My expectations for the class were minimal. I hoped only for a good grade at the end of the semester and maybe a few friends to help pass the time. So my hopes were the same as nearly every other student who walked through that door. At the end of my senior year, I was asked what class had the biggest impact on my high school experience and the answer was obvious. It was Mr. Sizemore's history class. History was still not my favorite subject. But as it turned out, it wasn't the subject matter that made the class great. It was Mr. Sizemore.

It's hard to put into words what made Mr. Sizemore such an amazing teacher. It was evident that he had a passion for what he taught and yet, it was also obvious that he knew what he taught was not the most important thing going on in the classroom.

Mr. Sizemore cared about his students, whether we had a passion for American History or not. And because of that, we actually ended up getting pretty fired up and discussing political topics of the past and present. He pushed us academically, and yet we always knew he believed that we could do what he was asking us to do.

Mr. Sizemore knew more about his students than most teachers did. He would greet us at the door each day and then spend time talking to us about the things we were interested in. He and I routinely broke down the strengths and weaknesses of our upcoming softball opponent. He attended extracurricular events to support his students. He encouraged us to take an active role in our school and use our gifts to make things better. He wanted us to excel at more than just his class. He wanted us to be successful in life.

Today I work in the field of education and spend a lot of time working with students with behavioral issues. I get the opportunity to collaborate with teachers and lead professional development sessions focusing on behavioral strategies and interventions. The need for support in working with kids is huge. These students are tough and our teachers are stretched too thin. And yet what I've learned in my professional career is what Mr. Sizemore lived daily. The most vital part of working with students is the relationship between the teacher and student. Without a strong relationship, the best behavioral tools will fail. But with a strong relationship, the possibilities are limitless. I honestly do not remember behavior issues arising in Mr. Sizemore's class. It was not because there were no difficult students in his class. The students respected Mr. Sizemore. And he respected us. Bad behavior did not have a place in that environment.

I will always be grateful for the opportunity I had to be a student in Mr. Sizemore's class and to truly learn from the best. And I even learned a few things about American History in the process.

Allison Bowsman
Valedictorian, Class of 2000

PREFACE

I met Lloyd Sizemore just a few weeks before we both started our first teaching assignments of our careers. That was in 1977 at a Junior High School in a northeastern suburb of Fort Worth, Texas. Having received a degree in Special Education and Biology from the University of North Texas, he was assigned to Resource Classes for 6th, 7th and 8th grade students in math and social studies – students with learning difficulties. He was also a member of the coaching staff there, a position he enjoyed after playing football at the high school to which the students of this junior high would soon attend.

The second year he was there, I was the cheerleader sponsor. But then I was also his wife. We both enjoyed teaching in the same school and investing together into the lives of those students for four years. There were, in fact, about seven married couples that were teachers at that school at the same time. In today's world, you probably would not find this a common practice. But there was a sense of family and it just seemed to work well for this group of students.

Lloyd was promoted to the high school from which he graduated at the beginning of his seventh year of teaching and never left until his retirement 29 years later. He coached there for several more years as good leadership qualities were being developed. After having two kids of his own, he decided to devote all of his time to being the best teacher he could be. So he stopped coaching. He served as the Social Studies department chair for 27 years, leading a group as large as some staffs of small schools. He taught several disciplines in the social studies department but his longest tenure and favorite subject was as an Advanced Placement (AP) American History teacher.

Mr. Sizemore did become the best teacher he could be! He was chosen the high school's Teacher of the Year for three different years during his 35 years as an educator. In 2002 and 2003, two different historical organizations named him "Outstanding American History Teacher for Tarrant County." In 2003, he was named the district's "High School Teacher of the Year." Ultimately, in 2011, he was inducted as the school's first teacher into the school's first Hall of Fame.

It was no accident that Mr. Sizemore was mentioned during many graduation ceremonies by top scholars who praised him for not only preparing them well for college but for the caring person that he was in their lives. Never was there a single report or rumor of inappropriate behavior about this teacher. He cared for his students' academic lives but had compassion for their everyday struggles. He is the father of four amazing adult children and four wonderful grandchildren (at this writing) who have loved and respected him to this day.

As his partner in life, in education and now as authors, I have learned tremendous lessons from him and have always admired the rewarding relationships that he built with his co-workers and especially with his students. He helped me stay grounded and aware of teacher struggles as I moved into school administration.

However, our entire family and his educational community were saddened when, after only two months into his retirement in August 2012, he suffered two serious strokes that changed all of our lives. He spent ten weeks in three hospitals before he was able to go home. Even once he was home, he needed constant assistance to take care of his basic needs. For eight more months, he spent eight hours every weekday at a rehabilitation center with speech, occupational and physical therapists. He received most of his nourishment through a feeding tube in his stomach for more than eight months. He was not able to drink anything but thick liquid for most of that time because he had lost the ability to swallow.

Thanks to modern medicine, technology, some amazing health care workers and therapists, he learned to speak again, to walk again and to take better care of himself. Our sons lived close to us and were so very helpful for that entire period of hospitalization and recovery. In fact, our middle son, Michael, who had just graduated from college put his plans on hold to stay at home and help me full time to take care of his dad for that year. I am forever grateful for his unselfish service and for their dedication and assistance to their dad. To this writing, they are still there for us anytime we need assistance!

I mention these details about Lloyd, his stroke and his hard-fought recovery to emphasize how incredible it is that he has his name as author on this book. Due to many continued disabling effects of his stroke, this book is a huge accomplishment. He is unable to write legibly due to tremors and he has never been able to drive since that night. But I am proud to assist him in the efforts that he has consistently put forth to write this book and to share the abundance of knowledge that he has for all those who aspire to be the best teachers they can be!

Thank you, dear Lloyd, for the example of your life as a great teacher, for the model you have shown to your children, for the proper and dedicated relationships that you had with your students and for being my companion in this life for over 40 years! You are greatly loved by your family and your educational community!

Your wife forever, Cheri

INTRODUCTION

My Path to Teaching

*What greater joy can a teacher feel than to witness
a child's success?*
~Michelle L. Graham

Smile before Christmas

The graduation exercises for the class of 2000 were underway at the cavernous Tarrant County Convention Center and part of those ceremonies included speeches by the honor graduates of the class. As a faculty member, I sat with the hundreds of graduates on the floor of the convention center. As the valedictorian of the class concluded her speech, she said, "I want to thank Lloyd Sizemore for showing that someone could be a teacher and a friend."

Reflecting back on the beginning of my career, I recall the first piece of advice I ever received regarding the student-teacher relationship. As part of teacher training before the school year began, our faculty had listened to a presentation regarding how to establish effective classroom management. After the presentation, we broke into small groups for discussion of classroom management techniques. In my group an experienced teacher immediately took control of the discussion. Shaking her finger at the new teachers, she told us that the way to manage kids was not to smile at our students until Christmas.

I spent the rest of the day and that night considering this advice and concluded that I had not worked full time while attending college for four years to become this type of teacher. My attitude toward developing positive teacher-student relationships was influenced by my own experiences as a student growing up.

What Do You Mean There is No Television?

My father was a career military man and was stationed in Ft Worth, Texas, when I began school as a first grader. The summer after my first year of school my parents shared with my sister and me that dad was being transferred to Italy for a four-year tour-of-duty. At the time, the only thing I knew about Italy was that it was the home of spaghetti - a food I enjoyed.

When my family arrived in Italy the following fall, we began to discover just how different our lives were going to be. This was many years before satellite television and, as such, there were no English language programs. As our television had been damaged beyond repair during the transit to our new home, my parents chose not to replace it. Instead, they purchased a large stereo with a record turntable, AM/FM radio and a short-wave radio. Over the coming years, we listened to a number of radio programs and collected a large number of albums of various types of music. I will always remember hearing the news of President Kennedy's assassination on that stereo.

In addition to music and radio programs, we passed our leisure time by playing a number of board games as a family. One of the perks of the assignment in Italy was going on guided tours offered by the base personnel to various historic sites. Reluctantly, I accepted my mother's insistence that we take part in these tours of ancient cathedrals, historic ruins and other notable attractions. Without realizing it, my lifelong romance with history began. Over the years, I came to believe that stories were one of the most effective means of communicating information to my students.

Books, Books and More Books

Another bonus that the military base offered to the families of the military personnel was the availability of affordable books – bundles of them sorted by age and interest. Each month when my parents traveled to the base to purchase groceries and other needs for our family, they began to purchase bundles of books for my sister and me. I was introduced to the exciting world of *The Hardy Boys*, written by Franklin W. Dixon. By the end of each month, I usually had read my way through the previous months' purchases. At the end of two years, I had collected a large library of books. We then received word that due to changes in America's NATO commitment, the small military installation in Italy was being closed and the remainder of my father's four-year tour would be in France.

France was both different and the same as daily life in Italy. Once again there was no English language TV for Americans. As a result, I devotedly continued my reading. I continued to read and collect books.

At the end of four years, my father's tour of duty in Europe ended and we found ourselves in Wichita, Kansas. We settled in a small, wheat-farming community (population: 150) outside of Wichita. My fourth-grade year passed without any major problem as I reintegrated into life in the United States.

Unfortunately for me, my fifth-grade teacher had apparently attended a workshop over the summer where a new instructional technique was introduced. This strategy involved a new way to evaluate students. When a new concept or instructional goal was introduced in a lesson, a day would be set aside for class questions and discussion. Each student received a grade based on the teacher's opinion of both the quantity and quality of student input to the discussion. There was on occasion a written assignment or quiz to aid in the assignment of grades for a grading period. Being a fairly typical fifth grade boy, I was often stuck for insightful comments to add to the class discussion.

I would encourage every teacher to utilize as many evaluation methods as possible. For example, I found that allowing students with artistic abilities to demonstrate their grasp of a topic was a perfectly effective way of evaluating student learning.

Oh, Lloyd! You and Your Books!

One day while the class discussion was whirling around me, it struck me that there were many examples from my readings that I could use to contribute toward my participation grade. For the next few months my grades rose due to my ability to call upon an almost unlimited supply of examples from various authors. But little did I know that this practice had apparently begun to wear thin with my teacher. I have never known if the teacher felt that I was "showing off" or what exactly bothered her in that she never brought a concern to me or to my parents.

The culmination came one day in the middle of a class discussion regarding a story character in English class. I had just made reference to an idea from *Treasure Island* that I was reading at the time. My teacher was at the front of the classroom. (This moment is still so vivid in my mind! I can recall exactly what she was wearing too!) She leaned over her grade book and in a voice dripping with contempt and disapproval announced to the entire class, "Oh, Lloyd! You and your books!"

Complete and Total Mortification

Needless to say, I was completely humiliated and that marked the end of my involvement in class discussions. Consequently, my grades began to fall. I found that part of effective classroom management and positive relationship building involved never calling out students in front of their peers. If a student required correction, I always made it a point to deliver that reprimand either in the hall or after class in order to avoid unnecessary embarrassment and potential conflict with students. At the end of the year when the district administered tests to determine student progress, my scores indicated that I had made little or no progress that year.

A Change of Scenery and Philosophy

The following year my dad retired from the military and we settled in what would become the first permanent home of my life – Ft. Worth, Texas. I was once again the new kid in the school. I dealt with that loneliness by spending a great deal of time at the local library that I passed each day while walking home from school. I muddled through the next few years of school not knowing that I was going to soon meet a teacher who would help change my life.

Why a Book on Wildlife?

During my years in school, textbooks for English classes were typically divided in half. The first half of the book was usually devoted to grammar and the rules of the English language. The other half of the book consisted of a collection of short stories and a novel of some type. As soon as our literature books were issued to us, I would immediately flip to the short stories and the novel and begin reading. I continued to read through my early teen years, but most of the reading material did not fall into the classics category. But that was going to change very soon!

My English teacher for my junior year in high school was an elderly, somewhat eccentric teacher with a good number of years of experience under her belt. A few weeks into the year, I continued my practice of reading short stories mixed in with library books in class when I could steal the opportunity. One day I was reading when I was supposed to be working on an assignment. When my teacher walked by my desk, she placed a book on my desk, tapped it with her finger and said, "I think you should read this." Caught off guard, I only glanced at the book as I returned to the written assignment. I was somewhat surprised as I saw the title of the book and thought to myself, "Why does she think I would be interested in a book about wildlife or hunting?" I then stored the book in my book bag along with my notebooks, pens and papers.

All Night Long

That night after dinner, I retreated to my room to do homework and to read. While rummaging through my bag, I pulled out the book my teacher had suggested that I read. I glanced at the title once again and opened to the first page of *To Kill a Mockingbird*. I quickly realized that this was no wildlife or sportsman book, as I became hypnotized by the tale of Atticus Finch and his family.

The sky was beginning to glow pink as I turned to the last page of what I discovered later was an American classic. I returned the book to Mrs. Freeman that day. She was surprised and asked if I had already read the book. When I confirmed that I had stayed up all night reading, she seemed pleased as she handed me another book. She said, "Well, if you liked that book, you should enjoy this one as well."

I was too tired to stay up all night and read this new selection, but I did finish it in just a few days. Once again, I was captivated by the tale of the Joad family. My parents were both from Eastern Oklahoma farm families during the Great Depression and I realized that *The Grapes of Wrath* could easily be a retelling of my family history. These two Great Books opened my eyes to a world of great literature that had not been familiar to me until then.

For the remainder of the year, Mrs. Freeman introduced me to other great writers by urging me to read George Orwell, Ayn Rand and the works of several other notable authors. Mrs. Freeman had taken the time to observe and realize that I had a love of reading and used that desire to read to teach me new ideas and ways of looking at the world.

I am extremely grateful to this day to Mrs. Freeman for being aware of my learning needs. To this very day, I continue to have several books at various stages of being read at the same time! There are books in every room of my house and that continues to be comforting to me!

Who Was Your Favorite Teacher?

In preparation to write this book, I took advantage of a great amount of time spent in travel that took me to both coasts and to Chicago. I made it a habit to ask fellow passengers to recall their days as students. Many were asked if they could recall a favorite teacher and the impact they had on them. Time and time again these "former students" showed little hesitation in answering my query. Almost without exception, I was told that this particular teacher made a difference because he or she made them feel that the teacher really cared about them.

One conversation in particular has always stuck with me. We were flying to Chicago to visit my daughter.

The seat beside me was unoccupied until right before we took off. A young lady carrying a heavy load in a backpack dashed through the door and took that seat. After the plane was airborne, everyone sat back to relax for the duration of the flight. Some donned headphones to listen to music; others opened books to pass the time; some, like me, tried to catch a quick nap. The young lady next to me rummaged through her backpack and extracted a large, hardback book and a spiral notebook. Soon she was busily scribbling complex chemical formulas while I attempted to see the title of the book. Eventually, I read the title, *Organic Chemistry.*

When she paused for a few minutes, I asked where she was going to school. I also asked her my favorite question: Did she have a favorite teacher? She proudly shared that she was a pre-med major at Southern Methodist University (SMU). The most influential teacher in her life was a 7th grade history teacher who, in her words, "really invested in the lives of his students." He organized tours of historic sites for his classes and acted as the tour guide. He also held special study sessions after school and on the weekends. I found her use of the phrase "investing in his students" interesting in that the idea of investing is typically used to denote placing

28

money in a business or fund in hopes of making a profit. In talking to this highly motivated and dedicated college student about her desire to become a physician, I have no doubt she will be an outstanding doctor. On any day that she helps a patient, her favorite teacher will have shown a profit on his investment in the lives of his students!

Why I Wrote This Book

Some people have asked me why I wrote this book. Many have been curious about the title's meaning. The subtitle, *10 Strategies for Building Positive Teacher-Student Relationships,* indicates the suggestions that I want to offer to teachers as they work to build good relationships with their students. With the title, *Teacher, Why Can't You Hear Me Raising My Hand,* I hope to raise some awareness of the plight that the American education system has faced for many years. The public school system of this country has repeatedly been used as a scapegoat for some problems facing this nation.

In the 1950's and 1960's, there was a great deal of national angst and soul searching to explain why the United States had seemingly fallen behind the Soviet

Union in space technology and missile expertise as illustrated by the launch of Sputnik. What was a political issue became an educational one when a government investigation concluded that the problem was the failure of schools to adequately prepare our students in math and science education. Almost immediately a great deal of legislatively mandated monies began to flow to public schools to boost the teaching of these two subjects. This amounted to an unspoken admission that our schools were not being sufficiently funded.

In the 1970's, public education became one of the centerpiece issues for a businessman-turned-politician seeking higher office. This marked the birth of the standardized test movement in this country as a solution to our perceived educational shortcomings.

As we entered the 21st century, our schools became cash cows for companies seeking to gain a foothold in the lucrative creation, distribution, and grading of all kinds of standardized tests. In my last year of teaching, our school test coordinator revealed to me that of the 185 days of school that year, a standardized test of some nature was being given on 80 of those days somewhere in the building, resulting in numerous hours of lost instructional time. While vast sums of money are being spent on testing, my own state made the decision to trash many millions of dollars worth of test supplies after it was discovered one year that the wrong tests had been distributed to many campuses across the state.

While these public monies were being thrown away, studies from school districts across the nation continue to reveal the declining infrastructure of our public schools – crumbling, aging schools, inadequate or poorly maintained restrooms, seriously inadequate heating and ventilation systems, and broken windows.

While these shortcomings in the renovation or repair of our children's schools continue, school districts across my home state regularly spend tens of millions of dollars on new football stadiums with artificial grass and jumbo replay screens that would be the envy of most college football programs. In many districts, school officials watch the games in glassed-in, air-conditioned comfort while enjoying catered meals at district expense. The parents and fans meanwhile sit in the heat and cold while paying for unreasonably high-priced cold chicken sandwiches and stale popcorn.

I chose to write this book at this time because our country is at a crisis point in education because of the 2020 pandemic's effect on our public school students. Multitudes of children have missed a significant portion of their foundational knowledge due to school closings. Children have been deprived of the opportunity to seek out knowledge and counsel because of the absence of teachers from their lives.

Our misplaced priorities and lack of enlightened leadership are subjecting our children to what I would characterize as intellectual poverty – a failure to be prepared for their future due to no fault of their own.

These errors in leadership have become increasingly difficult to address as the central office of many schools utilize a type of administrative praetorian guard to prevent parent or student communication with district leadership. I have come to believe that each member of the central office should be required to know the backstory of students and parents whose lives are impacted by their decisions. So, where do we go from here? How do we fix this increasingly broken system? I have felt and continue to believe that our country must find a way to attract our best and brightest to careers in education.

I am reminded of a conversation I once had with a district official regarding an upcoming bond proposal by the district. It had been revealed the leadership role in planning and leading the bond effort was to be given to an administrator who was notorious for his poor decision making skills. When I expressed concern that such an important job was being assigned to someone of such poor reputation, the only reply I received was a shoulder shrug and the discouraging endorsement of "Well, we all know that he makes a number of poor decisions, but he is the only person who is willing to make a decision."

As to making teaching a more attractive option to young people, I was recently told of a teacher who supplemented his income as an Uber driver in New York City. One evening his fare was a group of tourists vacationing from one of the northern European nations. After a few minutes of casual conversation, the visitors were almost incredulous that a teacher would need to work a second job. In their homeland, they told him, a teacher is a highly regarded and comparatively well-paid professional.

Not only must we find a way to improve pay for teachers, but we must find a way to keep them in the classroom. I recall that it took almost five years of teaching experience before I was totally confident in what I was doing. Because of this, I would also suggest that teachers must have a minimum of 5 years of classroom experience before applying for administrative positions.

Thank you for taking the time to read this book. I believe that by applying some of the strategies outlined in this book, teachers' classroom experiences will be much more pleasant ones. My hope is that more teachers will stay in the classroom so schools will not have to replace experienced teachers. So read on as I truly hope this will be an enjoyable and educational experience for you!

We Get One Chance to Get It Right

Schools do not have the ability to recall students to repair shortcomings in their education due to misplaced priorities. As I outline my strategies and beliefs, I would suggest parents to encourage that their local schools adopt these concepts as part of their teacher education programs, especially for newer teachers. Because many people who enter teaching are intrinsically empathetic, these strategies will probably be natural and automatic in their lives and in the classroom. Others may need to learn these behaviors; fortunately, they are learnable.

Within the last few years, I came across a fascinating study that illustrated the values that both parents and students want for their schools. The UCLA School of Graduate Education conducted a study of American schools – urban, suburban and rural. The schools examined were affluent, poor, multi-ethnic, and homogeneous. The study revealed that parents and students want more than just intellectual development. "The school is also, in the eyes of parents and students, a nurturing, caring place." "The parents we encountered want their children to be seen as individuals and learners… their children want to be known as persons as well as students."

A Place Called School by John Goodlad is quoted. "Criticism by those who use schools is focused less on these schools than on the system of schooling, it appears. Perhaps this is just part of the general decline of faith in our institutions and especially the bureaucratic insensitivity they are perceived to represent. The local school principal and teachers are more easily reached than are board members, the superintendent, other administrators and supervisors in the central office. There has been some shift away from the proposition that schools are most likely to be changed by mandates and strategies emanating from Washington or state capitals" (Goodlad, 1984, preface). His book and the strategies outlined here reflect my belief that schools can be improved one positive teacher-student relationship at a time.

During my years in the classroom and interacting with thousands of students, I utilized a number of very deliberate strategies to build positive teacher-student relationships. I share my heart through my favorite lines in Simon & Garfunkel's *Sound of Silence!*

*"Here my words that I might
teach you;
Take my arms that I might
reach you!"*

LESSONS LEARNED

MY PATH TO TEACHING

1. It IS OKAY to smile before Christmas! Don't waste a minute establishing good relationships with your students!
2. Make your lessons so interesting with rich storytelling that your students will enjoy learning about your topic!
3. Encourage lifelong learning through reading!
4. Don't be a reason that a student shuts down his or her learning!
5. Know your students' interests, hobbies, and passions and use them to inspire learning! Relationship-building requires a willingness to listen to your students' personal stories and journeys!
6. Show gratitude to those who make you a better reflection of yourself and encourage future teachers to do the same!

$$1$$

STRATEGY ONE

Teaching Kids is Much More Than Educating Students

"When we honestly ask ourselves which person in our lives means the most to us, often it is those, who instead of giving advice, solutions or cures choose rather to share our pain and touch our wounds with a warm and tender hand. The friend who can be silent with us in a moment of despair or confusion, who can stay with us in an hour of grief or bereavement."
Henry J.M. Nouwen

The Joys of Being a Rookie Teacher

As a new teacher, I didn't enjoy the luxury of being assigned to a classroom inside the main part of the school building. Instead, I had a classroom outside in what was affectionately known as a "portable." A portable was the school district's quick solution to a rapidly growing student population. When a district is unable to afford to build permanent structures to house the overpopulation, a district is forced to purchase aluminum mobile homes and build wooden partitions, dividing the structure in half to create two classrooms. These mobile homes were not new and had seen a great deal of use possibly as places of residence prior to being purchased by the district. (I always suspected they had been used by the military to house prisoners of war during World War II until they were deemed unfit for human habitation.)

Portables were constructed of aluminum sheets affixed to a steel frame by bolts, screws or other types of fasteners. With age, the body of the building had loosened from the frame and the slightest breeze would create conditions similar to that of being inside a metal barrel being pounded by angry gods. I was provided a foundation for the story of my first huge teacher lesson.

Early in my career I met two students who had a profound and lasting impact on how I would view my students for the next thirty-five years. They caused me to realize that some students come from a world I would not recognize. As such, I made a vow that I would never view any students as weird or strange and, as such, I needed to be willing to reach into their worlds in order to truly be their teacher – in the classroom and in life.

I Think of Her When It Thunders

The first of about 4000 students I was to know in my career was a young lady named Sally. *(Note: The names of all students mentioned in this book have been changed to protect their real identities.)* One afternoon just a few days before the start of school, I had a knock on my classroom door. When I answered the door, I found a young lady who introduced herself as Sally and would be in my first period class. She shyly asked, "Are you Mr. Sizemore?" Sally was typical for a preteen girl who was trying to make the leap from childhood to adolescence. She was gangly – all elbows and kneecaps – and nature had thrown a handful of freckles across her nose and cheekbones. We chatted for a few minutes, but as a new teacher, I did not have the experience to recognize that Sally was carrying the burden of a world of emotional issues. But it did not take long for me to learn something very important and saddening about Sally.

On the third day of my brand new teaching career, the weather forecast called for severe storms in the area for that morning. Indeed, on my way to class I could already see the growing darkness on the western horizon along with occasional flickers of lightning. As I began class, the rumble of thunder became more and more audible. From my location in the front of the classroom, I could see that Sally was becoming visibly agitated. With each new clap of thunder, she would rearrange her books and papers on her desk and move her purse from one side of her desk to the other. (I should note that this was in a time when ladies' fashions were moving toward smaller purses; Sally carried what I would describe as a "grandma purse." My grandmother carried a purse large enough to hold camping supplies for a week, and that was like Sally's purse.)

As Sally became more agitated with the approach of the storm, I recognized her panic and began to move closer to her desk so that I might calm her with some reassuring words. Just as I arrived next to her desk, the storm fell upon my fragile, aluminum portable with a crashing and rattling assault that unnerved even me. At this same moment, Sally emitted a loud scream of terror and simply melted out of her desk onto the floor. She pulled her purse completely over her head and began to scream. I pulled a chair next to Sally's desk as she continued to scream with each new sound of thunder. After about fifteen minutes as the storm moved away, I was finally able to coax Sally from the floor and out from under her purse.

I had taken the mandatory Child Psychology classes as part of my degree in Education, but I recognized that I was dealing with a situation beyond my expertise. As I reflected on what I had witnessed, I realized that Sally demonstrated a terror of extraordinary depth. I knew that this was far beyond my feeble knowledge of emotional troubles and my ability to effectively handle. Later that day, I met with school counselor and asked if there was anything in Sally's permanent records that would explain her behavior.

The next day the counselor called me in and told me that there was nothing in Sally's file that would explain what had happened. The counselor had, however, contacted the counselor from Sally's previous school in hopes of finding the answers I was seeking. What we discovered was horrific and unbelievable. When Sally was in first grade, her father, in a fit of anger over some imagined wrongdoing, had attacked and beaten Sally with a hammer. The attack had left her with, not only learning difficulties and brain damage, but also deep psychological scars that would interrupt her learning throughout her many years of schooling ahead.

It was during my very first week of school that I understood that my job involved much more than teaching multiplication tables, the periodic chart or historical dates. This profound experience, although I was unaware at the time, laid a foundation that drove me to make it a top priority to know my students and to establish caring relationships with them.

I Think of Her When a Student Falls Asleep in Class

After three years of teaching, Cheri and I purchased our first home, and like many young couples, we discovered that we had more house than we had furniture to go in it. After much discussion, we agreed that I would get an extra job that summer in order to allow us to purchase the furnishings we desired. I applied for a job with the district teaching summer school. I was notified that I would be teaching Texas History to 7th graders who had just failed this class in the spring semester. It was continually stressed to me the importance of finding a way to get these students to pass this class in order that they might have enough credits to move on to 8th grade. Research had shown that students who fall behind their peers seldom catch up and the probability of dropping out of school goes up dramatically. In order to allow these student to take as many classes as possible, summer school began much earlier than the regular school year (7:00 A.M.) – early for even the most motivated and accomplished young people but almost beyond imagination for these students.

I began my first class amongst the expected grumbling and complaining of their summer break being "stolen." I had begun the necessary task of checking schedules and names for correct placement. After about 15 minutes, there was a wild pounding on my door. I opened the door to find a young lady named Rebecca, who seemed frantically put together for the day. While still out of breath, she attempted to apologize for her tardiness. I told her that it was okay because we were just getting organized. I invited her in and told her to pick any open desk. She carefully surveyed the room, spied an unoccupied desk in the far corner of the room, made her way back to it and collapsed into the seat. Within minutes, though, Rebecca was head down on the desk and fast asleep. For the next hour no amount of polite tapping, clearing my throat or literal shaking of her desk would arouse Rebecca from what seemed to be the sudden onset of a coma. Needless to say, Rebecca missed any and all instructions for the assigned work for the day. The following day, unsurprisingly, Rebecca had no completed work to turn in and so she started summer school history with a zero average. In addition to not having completed the previous day's assignment, she arrived 15 to 20 minutes late to class again. Upon entering class she once again fell into a deep sleep. Once again she completed no work for the day and fell further behind. This behavior repeated itself for two more days and at the end of the week I could see that Rebecca was heading toward a disastrous outcome in my class. Over the weekend, I decided that I was going to have to have some kind of intervention with Rebecca.

On the following Monday, when I began class Rebecca was not there and I sensed a certain amount of humorous expectation on the part of the class as they anticipated Rebecca's usual late arrival and "ghost walk" to her desk. She finally did arrive 15 minutes late and I asked her to step into the hall with me.

I explained that she would have to change her habits in order to pass this class. When I asked for an explanation for her habitual tardiness and inability to stay awake in class, she totally blew me away with an answer that I never imagined. She proceeded to tell me that she had a one-month-old baby who cried all night and prevented her from sleeping. I had not known of a pregnant classmate in high school so the idea of a thirteen-year-old being a mother of a month old baby was almost beyond my ability to believe.

Cheri and I had no children at this point so most of my knowledge of caring for a baby was mostly theoretical. In trying to determine why the child was crying all night, my first thought was hunger. "Are you feeding the baby before bedtime?" I asked. She assured me that she was. "Are you warming the bottle before the feeding?" She looked at me with an incredulous expression and asked, "Why would my baby want his Coca-Cola warmed up?" Even with my limited knowledge of babies, I was shocked.

I then asked Rebecca if her mother was providing help or guidance in caring for the baby. I was about to get my third shock in five minutes. In a rather embarrassed tone of voice, she told me that her parents, upon learning of the pregnancy, had kicked her out of their home. She admitted that she was now living in a government-assisted apartment. After catching my breath, I did secure a promise from Rebecca that she would stop giving her baby cola drinks.

For a few days, the situation took a turn for the better. Rebecca remained awake enough to complete a few assignments. But after the brief period of improvement, she fell back into her old bad habits. I once again had a private conference with her in the hall. I questioned her about what she was giving the baby before bed. "You are not feeding him Coca-Cola again, are you?" She quickly assured me that she had not because she promised me she would stop that practice. She then surprised me again when she explained that now she was giving him tea at bedtime. When I managed to pick my jaw up off of the floor, I contacted the summer administrators to see if some type of parental training and a milk provision was available to Rebecca.

As dark as this account is, Rebecca was supplied with the help she needed. I worked with her in creating a system that allowed her to complete her work beyond the deadline, while she was dealing with a problem at home. Her grades improved over time; she passed the summer class; and she moved on to eighth grade. The last time I saw Rebecca was on the day she received her high school diploma!

LESSONS LEARNED

TEACHING KIDS IS MUCH MORE THAN EDUCATING STUDENTS

1. Many teachers teach the way they were taught. Many probably went to school in an atmosphere different from what they face in their classrooms now. The challenge for today's teacher is to be able to connect with today's students to understand the challenges and difficulties of today's kids.

2. Educators sometimes sarcastically claim that being proficient in your teaching field is not a sufficient prerequisite for teaching today. Being proficient in your teaching field isn't always enough. The truly successful teacher must also have skills of a child psychologist and sociologist.

3. Teachers are instrumental in educating students about life. This includes teaching common sense, tolerance, compassion, sympathy, empathy, survival in society, and much more that is not necessarily included in educational curricula.

2

STRATEGY TWO

Making Connections

You can't stay in your corner of the forest waiting for others to come to you. You have to go to them sometime.
A. Milne, Winnie the Pooh

Names Are Important Too

On the first day of a new school year, many students struggle to their classes under the weight of countless notebooks, binders, pencils, pens, laptops and other school-mandated supplies. But many others don't have the means of taking these supplies, much less taking the newest tools and gadgets that their classmates have and teachers take for granted. A few bring only their names with them but that is an important possession.

For years as the chair of the Social Studies department, I had the opportunity to observe other classes in my department. I enjoyed observing different styles of teaching. However, it was always discouraging to hear a teacher refer to a student as "Hey, You" after six weeks of school. I can think of few things that more clearly send the message that "You are not important" than failing to learn your students' names after a reasonable period of time.

There are several easy strategies that can be used to facilitate the process of learning student names. In a technique I learned from my wife, I would stand at the door of my classroom between classes and as the next group entered, I would encourage them to shake my hand and introduce themselves.

It never ceases to amaze me how many adults have failed to learn this most basic of human interactions. So many adults try to impress you by crushing your hand or use the dreaded "dead fish" handshake.

Very soon, not only did I master my students' names, they mastered the art of a professional handshake. They also came to demand that I shake their hands each day. If I was distracted by a conversation and failed to see a student waiting for their handshake, they began to make it a point to stand in my sightline and loudly clear their throat to signal my neglect of their greeting.

Another technique was to return graded papers by calling the students' name and have them come to my desk to take the paper from my hand. Students always seemed amazed that I could greet them by their names in the halls or in the cafeteria.

The importance of learning student names was driven home to me a few years after my retirement. One morning my wife and I had some early morning errands to run and while out, we stopped into a restaurant to grab a quick breakfast. When we entered the shop, I recognized a former student who was working there. I greeted her by her name and asked how she was doing. A few minutes later the young lady moved from behind the counter, came to our table and, with tears streaming down her face, gave me a huge hug and said, "I can't believe you remember my name." While this strategy may seem trivial, it does effectively send the message to students that they are important.

I prided myself for having a "mental Rolodex" of several thousand of student names in my head. Unfortunately, only two months after I retired, I suffered two severe strokes in a day and a portion of my brain was greatly affected and many of those names were erased forever. I continually mourn the loss of those names and so many memories that were connected to them.

Know Your Supervisors and Administrators

During most of my tenure as a teacher, a wonderful educator led my district. Dr. Jay Thompson and I had a long relationship based on mutual interests and experiences. Whenever he happened to be in my building for some school-related business, he would make it a point to drop by my classroom to visit with my students. He would quietly slip into the class and without disrupting the learning process would talk to the kids about what they were learning that day. After a few minutes, he would once again quietly leave the classroom. Kids would always ask, "Who was that guy?' When I explained that he was the assistant superintendent for the district, the kids would exclaim, "Wow, we don't think we've ever seen one of them." This comment always saddened me just a little because these were students who had attended our schools for eleven years. The concept that our leadership was so unrecognizable and remote from our students troubled me.

As important as the name is to the child, we have to understand who the child is behind the name.

You Often Don't Realize Your Impact

In the last few years of my career, I had a student who died in a tragic car accident. A few weeks after her death, her mother sent me a large number of texts and emails that her daughter had shared with a friend from another school. I was stunned to see that I was mentioned specifically as someone the student trusted implicitly. I wasn't sure what I had done to warrant this level of trust and admiration, but unknowingly I must have. We may not always be aware of the impact that we are having on the life of a student. For better or worse, we must always keep in mind that we have a significant role in a student's life.

Challenges Facing Relationships

One of the most pressing issues facing teacher-student relationships is that many children are not going to class. Chronic absenteeism or missing at least 10% of school days are increasingly common among students, especially during a pandemic. Poor attendance can be a predictor of later dropout potential. Additionally, it becomes nearly impossible to build a relationship with a student the teacher rarely sees. It seems that a growing number of public school students are dealing with traumatic experiences in their lives, which would limit the ability of the teacher to build this relationship. The importance of these relationships are key as research has shown by the resulting increased academic achievement of students and promotion of self-motivation, while at the same time, decreasing chronic absenteeism.

Did They Call Her Mom?

A number of my students have gone on to be teachers themselves, including several who taught my own children. As I recognized in my children's education some of the very methodologies and techniques that I utilized in teaching their teachers, there was a sense of deep satisfaction that the lessons learned and passed on to others were in small part helping to change lives.

My wife taught two of our sons in her Pre AP Geometry classes in another school. It was definitely an interesting situation and all three survived those years. Although the boys occasionally were teased or accused of being able to use the teacher's edition of the textbook, they might have, in fact, experienced a higher level of expectation from their mother than other class members. It is interesting, to this day, to see the relationship and respect that they show their mother and former teacher. By the way, one of my sons did call her Mom in class. It is my understanding that the other one never said much at all!

LESSONS LEARNED

MAKING CONNECTIONS

1. While popularity is not the ultimate goal for a teacher, I found that the teachers who were both respected and well liked by their students tended to be among the most effective teachers in the school and the most popular too.

2. Over the years since I retired, a number of students have contacted me visa Facebook and started their messages with the words, "I know you probably don't remember me. but…" And when I am able to reassure them that I can, their reactions are usually one of amazement. Too often it seems as if our system concentrates on herding our children for twelve years as if they are cattle to be moved from one point to another. Know their names. Get to know them as people.

3. In this soulless quest for higher test scores and graduation rates, we too often ignore the human side of our profession.

3

STRATEGY THREE

Listen More Than You Talk

You can talk to someone for years, every day, and still, it won't mean as much as what you can have when you sit in front of someone, not saying a word, yet you feel that person with all of your heart, you feel you know that person, for connections are made with the heart and not the tongue.
C. Joy Bell

Pick Up the Details and Use Them

In this era of standardized testing, educators face a huge challenge to reclaim the caring, nurturing mission of educators. I understand that standardized tests are useful for school districts to justify large administrative salaries and tax increases because test scores are easier to judge rather than teacher impact on students.

I made a habit of creating lesson plans calling for group work as often as I could. While the students were working in groups, I would walk among the groups to monitor their work. When the opportunity presented itself, I would sit with a group and talk to individual students. In our conversations, I would ask what hobbies or interests they had and in what extracurricular activities they were involved. Sometimes they shared the name of their boyfriend or girlfriend. I also asked what their goals were after high school graduation.

Help Her, Encourage Her – Then Celebrate

Carla, a well-liked, personable, young lady confided very quietly with some obvious degree of embarrassment that she wanted to go to college – something that no one in her family had ever done. She went on to explain that she didn't think this would be possible, though, because her parents could not afford for her to attend college.

The next day I met with Carla and made a commitment to her that if she really wanted to go to college, I would do what I could to facilitate that goal. Throughout the next year, when Carla had moved on to other classes, we continued to meet on a regular basis to check her grades and to clarify what college she might want to attend. I wrote letters to admissions officers and grant and scholarship advisors on an almost weekly basis.

One day in late spring as graduation approached, Carla dashed into my room, waving an envelope and chanting, "I did it! I did it!" When I asked what had happened, Carla explained that she had been accepted into a small college and that there would be sufficient funds available for her. I gave her a quick hug around the shoulders and told her how proud I was of her. She immediately burst into tears and I was afraid that I had "crossed a line." She quickly explained that she could not remember when someone in her life had given her a hug and told her that they were proud of her.

This was a young lady who was well liked, an outstanding student, and a sweet person, and yet there was no one in her life who was willing to acknowledge her worth or who had the knowledge to support her college interest. A few years later, I received a college graduation announcement from Carla to let me know that she had received her degree.

Form Sincere Bonds

One year I had several classes that I felt that I had established genuine bonds with certain students. The church that I attended with my family had announced that they were encouraging members to invite friends to a special "friends-day service." I made an announcement in several classes that any student who was interested in joining me was invited to attend this service as a friend of mine. And furthermore, they were also invited to lunch at our home. Much to my surprise when the day arrived, over two dozen of my students, each neatly pressed and looking their very best, arrived at the church. They filled two pews and the members expressed to me their amazement that these students desired to attend with their teacher. I had made it very clear that I was not attempting to proselytize any of the students to my denomination or church. All those who chose to attend were to get their parents' approval before attending.

After the service, most of them came to our house and I grilled hamburgers for everyone. We spent the afternoon exchanging stories and laughing about events that had occurred in class. To this day, I occasionally cross paths with members of this group when I am in the community or on social media. They never fail to mention the day that they attended church with me and I fed them hamburgers afterwards.

Demonstrate Sensitivity

We need to keep in mind our own experiences with teachers in our past that helped open up a world of understanding and learning by their willingness to reach out to their students. Conversely, for each of these positive experiences, students may have endured negative experiences with a teacher. Such was my earlier account of an extremely gifted African American fourth grade classmate, named Daniel, who was relegated to a learning group titled, the "black birds" by the teacher. No matter how many high scores he achieved each grading period, he was confined to the black bird group instead of being elevated to the predominantly white students within the class that had been labeled blue birds, cardinals and robins. During recess, I would play with him and we became best friends. I was aware of the looks and thoughts of some of my classmates and teachers. Even though I was in elementary school, I was amazed that he was not embittered by his treatment at the hands of "responsible adults."

When I recently participated in a local "Black Lives Matter" march, I could not help but think of my friend from years ago and the many other students of color that I had witnessed being judged and mistreated by an educational system that was seemingly rigged against them.

Part of the relationship-building process is the willingness to accept and acknowledge previous wrongs by teachers in a student's life. We must be willing to listen to and understand how these negative experiences can impact student learning over succeeding years. Even though I attended public schools that were considered to be in "progressive school districts," students of color had been, in previous years by policy, excluded from enrolling in the schools I attended.

Be Sincere When You Listen

I was always curious to know how the students viewed the structure of my class, so I would do my own internal survey at the end of each year. I questioned the students regarding what they liked about the year, how they reviewed the way that I taught and what they felt would make the next year even better. My survey indicated that there were a number of subjects within the curriculum they expressed they wanted to learn more about, such as more about Vietnam in the sixties. They expressed frustration with the detailed minutia found in the course curriculum. Remembering the struggle that I sometimes encountered in college to recall small bits of information, I gave my students permission to use highlighters in their textbooks to aid their studies. This worked to the students' advantage as they had the benefit of seeing what information that the previous students who used the book felt was noteworthy.

LESSONS LEARNED

LISTEN MORE THAN YOU TALK

1.   When a construction contractor sets out to build a home, he does it deliberately by following a blueprint or a set of plans.   In the same way, building positive relationships with your students requires a deliberate intention and plan. Find your plan. Follow your plan.

2. Listening to students' passions outside of the classroom opens avenues for instruction inside the classroom. It also allows you the opportunity to build more sincere relationships with your students.

3.   As our society becomes more and more complex and parents struggle to provide financially, many are forced to take second jobs and work long overtime hours. The result is that the students often have no adult figure consistently present from whom to seek advice. *En loco parentis* is today, more than ever, applicable in our current society as teachers take on many tasks as "substitute parents."

4

STRATEGY FOUR

Don't Judge a Book By Its Cover

Our lives end the day we become silent about the things that matter.
Martin Luther King, Jr.
****

I follow three rules: do the right thing, do the best you can, and always show people you care.
~Lou Holtz

Focus on the Important Stuff

Like most school districts, the one in which I taught for over three decades had strict policies about what students could wear and how they were expected to look. Dress

Codes are open invitations for student rebellion against the established norms. Our district clearly spelled out the rule for the students' hair color and style.

The district claimed that any deviation from one's "natural hair color" was "disruptive to the learning process." However, wearing a splash of color in their hair became a popular trend in society; thus, students started following this trend. On those occasions when a student with an "out-of-compliance" hairstyle managed to slip past an administrator into a classroom, the other students barely raised their eyebrows. No riots or pandemonium broke out as a result of someone choosing to challenge the norm.

To demonstrate the hypocrisy of the enforcement of this rule, consider this situation that presented itself. The varsity football team had qualified for the playoffs and to celebrate this achievement, every member of the team bleached their hair a bright, unnatural blond. I pointed out to an administrator that this violated the district policy on hair color – a rule that this assistant principal usually delighted in enforcing. He responded by telling me that this was acceptable because it was for school spirit.

One year, I had a young man who was African American – a fine student with no disciplinary issues and a member of several sports' programs. One day he came into the class visibly upset. When asked what was wrong, he explained that an administrator had detained him because of his hairstyle. I could not see any difference from how he usually wore it. When asked what was wrong with it, he told me that he had gotten a "faux-hawk" with a strip of hair about two inches wide and about one-quarter inch taller than the surrounding hair. Unless he got another haircut that afternoon, he would be removed from all extracurricular activities.

The district also had a firm policy on students displaying tattoos of any type. The students were infuriated by the fact that a member of the administration openly flouted a tattoo.

What is Best for the Student?

An academically challenged student signed up for my AP class. One day he got in trouble in another class and was to be assigned to in-school-suspension for two weeks. This would keep him from receiving any valuable instruction for two whole weeks. I did not have any problems with this student so I approached the administration with a plan to allow him to stay in my class ALL day for the next ten days of school. His assignments from other classes were sent directly to me. I gave him a different assignment during each class period and kept an eye on him to see that he completed them. At the end of two weeks, he had completed all of his work, stayed current with my class and did not cause me one bit of problem. How did he do in my class by the end of the year? He passed, although I offered extra help for him.

Listen to Your Heart

As was my custom, I was standing at the threshold of my classroom, I was trying to gauge the level of enthusiasm and positivity. In other words, I was trying to "read the room." The last student who entered the class was a young lady who was normally well dressed with an upbeat attitude. On this particular day, Michelle appeared to me to be visibly downtrodden and uncharacteristically glum. During the lesson which included group work, I noticed that she was not participating in the conversation.

When the class ended, I made a point to ask if she was okay. After a moment's hesitation and somewhat ashamedly, she told me that her stepfather was trying to have sex with her. I took her immediately to our crisis counselor and informed her of the situation. I watched as child welfare and the local police were called and arrived at the office. At that point, I felt the situation was in the appropriate hands and would be well handled. The next day I was informed that Child Welfare had removed Michelle and her younger brother from the house, with the arrest of her stepfather imminent. When she returned to the class in a few days, she shared that she would miss some time while she was a witness in her stepfather's trial.

She requested her classwork so she could stay current with her assignments. After a couple of weeks, Michelle returned to class with a withdrawal form for me to sign. I asked her where she was going. She told me that the judge and Child Welfare would no longer allow her and her brother to live in the same house as her mother and stepfather. When given a choice of moving out from her husband or giving up child custody, Michelle's mother chose to give up custody. I was crushed by this news. For weeks and now years, I have questioned my decision to follow through with this concern.

DON'T JUDGE A BOOK BY ITS COVER

1.   My own children delight in teasing me about the platform shoes and the length of my hair in the seventies. We all have gone through phases where others have looked at us thinking, "How could they ever be taken seriously?" Be careful in labeling students as failures just by the way they look or the social status from which they come.

2. Before making a judgment of students by the way they do or say something, get to know them better, talk with the parents, and drive through their neighborhoods. You may discover that they are doing their very best. Show empathy, care and concern and offer to meet them halfway.

3. Build up your students when you can as opportunities arise. Self-esteem can be destroyed or enhanced by the way you respond. Function as if you may be the nly one giving positive strokes.

5

STRATEGY FIVE

Become An Advocate For Your Students

Never be afraid to raise your voice for honesty and truth and compassion against injustice and lying and greed. If people all over the world would do this, it would change the earth.
~William Faulkner

We Are All Here for the Students

My school district increasingly built a number of firewalls and obstacles to discourage parents and teachers from contacting district decision-makers. A new superintendent had been hired and he made an initial visit to our school. As he was making his way down our hall, a colleague of mine planned to introduce himself and shake hands with the new leader. As my friend approached the superintendent with outstretched hand, he was ushered to the side by a building administrator, with the admonition, "He doesn't have time to talk to anybody." That attitude made me wonder if the leadership would ever have time to speak to kids and to the people who made a difference in the lives of these kids. I questioned his visit that day.

Speak Up When You See Something Wrong

From time to time, I was reminded what one of my job descriptions should be: To reach out to those who need an advocate in their time of need. Abby approached me one day and shared with me that she was pregnant and would be leaving school until the baby was born. During the time that she was away from school, a homebound teacher would pick up her weekly assignments and would meet with her at her home to help with school work. She explained that her mother was willing to help with the baby so she could finish school. She very much wanted to go to college so that she could provide a decent life for her child.

She was dedicated to completing her work each week to be returned to me. After I graded each week's work, I would write her a short note expressing my well wishes for her and her baby. After a few weeks, I received a note back from her indicating that one of her teachers was refusing to send her work. It was my understanding that this refusal to provide her work was based on the teacher's personal disapproval regarding her pregnancy.

I had known this teacher for a number of years and considered her not only a colleague but a friend as well. When I visited with the teacher, I was surprised at the angry outburst directed at the student. When she pointed out that, in her opinion, the girl should never have gotten pregnant. I pointed out the obvious though – that she had. She continued in her tirade about why she had no business raising this child even with her mother's help. This teacher saw no reason to encourage this kind of behavior by helping her. I responded by telling her that we all had an obligation to help this student – an opinion that she angrily rejected.

On behalf of Abby, I approached the principal for an intervention. The principal did step in and the student received the assignments from the teacher.

Over a period of years, I received correspondence from Abby when she graduated from college and when she took her own daughter to college as a freshman. This put a smile on my face each time and I was grateful to have been able to help her when she needed it.

Show Empathy

Torn jeans and frayed jeans were also against the Dress Code policies. When my wife served as a middle school assistant principal, a young man was sent to the office for wearing pants that had been cut off at the bottom and were not hemmed. When she examined the young man's discipline file, she discovered that he had been written up several times by the same teacher for wearing this same pair of pants. My wife, who was very good at digging into the root of student behavior, asked the young man, "Why do you keep wearing those pants if you know you are going to get in trouble?"

His story was heartbreaking but not an unusual situation. He explained that the pants were too long for him and his mother "hemmed" them with a pair of scissors. He continued to wear them because they were the only pair of pants that he owned. That evening Cheri related this story to me. I knew that this had really touched her heart. She said, "I did something today and I hope you will not be upset." After school she went to a local thrift store and purchased four pair of pants in this boy's size to give to him the next day. Although we had four children of our own to clothe, we knew it was an important and necessary thing to do for this family.

Other than these dress code violations, this young man had no other disciplinary incidents. I have tried to imagine the dread that he must have felt each day when pulling on the frayed pants, knowing he might be sent to the office again. I have to question what lesson was branded into this boy's psyche and what lesson was imparted by the judging of his family's inability to provide clothing equal to that of his peers? How much had he been bullied because of his unfortunate life situation? Why should it matter enough to pull a student out of instructional time?

Show Compassion

This is not a one-time incident. Teachers all over the world dip into their own pockets to help the students who have great needs. Some teachers provide snacks for kids who do not eat breakfast. My wife continued to do what she could do to help kids whose families were struggling. For one, she established a meal account when she served as an assistant principal and continued as a principal. She was constantly observing to see which students did not have enough money in their accounts or had no lunch at all. She would go to the cafeteria worker who was checking out the kids. "Put it on the 'principal's account,'" she would quietly tell her. She shared with me that she had this account and also shared that very little of it was ever repaid. She never expected that kind of return on her investment.

Another example was thanks to the uniform policy for which my wife's middle school received school board approval. The first year that they began this program, they were able to work a deal with a company to provide three complete outfits for students for a very minimal cost to parents. As the second year approached, students who were moving to the high school were encouraged to donate their sets of clothes. For that year and succeeding years, the school had gently-worn uniforms available (free of charge) to the families who could not afford to purchase them. In addition, during the year, as students outgrew or needed an extra pair of pants or a shirt, my wife could fit them with clothes from the collected stash. Although there originally was some push back regarding uniforms, the parents soon realized the service that the school was offering while raising the pride and improving the behavior of the students in that building.

It is sometimes a mystery to those in authority why students are so defiant toward their policies. This is why it is vital that we all listen to what our students have to say – and often it is through nonverbal language. Listening allows us to know the rest of the story and to put things into perspective.

Step in When Needed

In some school communities in which many parents often have two or more jobs, students must attend school programs, fine arts events or recognition ceremonies without any family support. I made a real effort to attend as many of the extracurricular events that I could. Often my own children and wife joined me. It is important for students to know that they are supported in the extra things to which they have committed. The students notice when you are there. You may not only be an observer in the audience; you may be there as a student's advocate, standing in for a family member who is otherwise unable to attend.

Like most high schools in Texas, the one I spent a majority of my career had a drill team that performed at half time of football games. One of the highlight performances for the drill team was a father/daughter routine. Toward the end of my career, I was approached by several of the officers of the drill team who were also my students. They explained that they had a favor to ask of me. One member of the team did not have a father in her life and as a result had no one to perform with her as a partner. They asked if I would be willing to stand in as this young lady's father for that father/daughter dance. I was at first hesitant as I lacked even the smallest amount of dancing DNA in my entire make up. I was assured that this was no problem, as we would practice the dance routine for a couple of weeks after school. Based on the promise that they would help me in whatever way was necessary, I agreed to their request.

The next few weeks were a blur of missteps and spins for me as we practiced, as my pretend daughter worked patiently with me. As the big night approached, I found myself combating a growing swarm of butterflies. My family gathered together on the sidelines to video my performance. I was sure to give them a humorous conversation piece for years to come. Despite my fears, I managed to get through the routine without a memorable pratfall. At the end of the dance, my partner and I exchanged a quick hug as I said goodbye to my new friend.

Compromise When They Are Hurting

The next story involves a young lady who was being defeated by the circumstances of life. The young lady in this story seemed to have everything in life going for her. She was popular, outgoing and usually came to class well prepared for the days work. On a particular day, several assignments from the day before were due. After I collected the homework, I saw that Sarah had failed to turn in any of the assignments. I asked her to stay after class so I could discuss her failure to do the assigned work. One of the advantages of experience in the classroom is that over time you begin to develop a type of sixth sense when a student is being truthful or not. When I questioned Sarah as to the reason for not completing her work, she told me that she was looking after her younger brother and this included cooking dinner for him and doing the family laundry. I then made a mistake by asking a question for which there was no good answer in this situation. I simply asked, "Where was your mom while you were having to do all of these chores?" Without a second's hesitation and with perfect honesty that left no doubt she was telling the truth, she replied. "She was out bar hopping – looking for men." I was stunned to my core, but tried not to show it. I worked out a schedule and a contingency plan for her to get her work turned in. I also made it known that she should keep me informed if she found herself in a similar circumstance again. My job as a teacher not only included lesson planning but identifying and meeting the needs of my students.

"Yet, taught by time, my heart has learned to glow for other's good and melt at other's good."

Homer

LESSONS LEARNED

BECOME AN ADVOCATE FOR YOUR STUDENTS

1.   Schools, like many institutions, can fall prey to prejudice and favoritism. Parents may have difficulty maneuvering through the bureaucracy of the school. So it often becomes the responsibility of the teacher to step forward and speak for the children's rights and needs.

2.   By trusting the students with what may seem like small issues, this practice may lead to trust on larger, more difficult issues or problems. Opening this two-way trust system may allow students to approach you with problems and seek your help. They might otherwise feel too embarrassed and frightened to confide in you.

3.   There are often students who, because of their desires to follow the rules, will take the abuse or disciplinary actions given to them without an argument or discussion. It is critical that teachers make the time to ask questions and to listen with their hearts in order to discover the underlying reasons for things that are happening. If no one else, teachers should advocate for these shy students on behalf of their humanity and fair treatment.

87

6

STRATEGY SIX

Be the Best You Can Be ... Always!

When you encourage others, you in the process are encouraged because you are making a commitment and difference in a person's life.
~Zig Ziglar

She Taught Me about Life Too

Lessons on how to be a better teacher can come from the most unexpected places. One day just a few days after the start of a new school year, my classroom phone rang. I answered it to hear the voice of the head counselor. She made a request for a favor. She explained that she knew that I already had a full class in my sixth period but she asked if would I consider squeezing in one more student? Another teacher in my department said that she did not feel equipped to work with this student. I agreed to take on the additional student.

Minutes after my last class had departed, there came a weak knock on my door. When I opened the door, Angie was there in a motorized wheelchair. She was wearing a knitted skullcap with tiny strands of her hair protruding from underneath. She wore glasses that were almost as thick as any I had ever seen. An oxygen tank was attached to the chair and a tube ran from the tank to her nose. I invited her into my room and offered a place for her to sit close to my desk. She introduced herself and I began trying to get her up to speed on what she had missed the first few days of class.

Angie was in a very frail state physically. A teacher's aide was eventually assigned to accompany her to each class to provide her assistance. I discovered that in the previous year, Angie had won an award for best female athlete in her school and had been one of the top students in her class. During the summer, however, doctors detected a brain tumor that was steadily stealing her life.

There was something about Angie that caused the other girls in the class to open their hearts to her. They made sure that she received her papers and were always eager to help her. Interestingly, this particular class had what I considered a fairly rough group of female students. But to their credit, whenever the girls were talking about boys and the things teenage girls talk about, they always made room for Angie and made sure she was included in their chat sessions.

As the semester wore on, I could tell the disease was taking its toll on Angie. Her eyesight was continuing to decline and she seemed to be on the verge of exhaustion on a daily basis. A few days before the school was scheduled for the fall break, I sat with Angie and suggested that she might take a few days off to recover her strength. She eyed me carefully and in her raspy, gasping voice told me, "I want to be like the other kids as long as I can." A few days into our break, I received the phone call that I had been expecting and dreading all the same. In another few days, I found myself standing at a memorial service for Angie with her knit skullcap in front of me. This brave, strong person had reminded me why it was so important that I bring my best effort to class each day. If a student like Angie was going to struggle to continue to learn no matter what, she deserved the very best teacher everyday.

Offer Your Best Lessons for Your Students

My wife gave me the title early in our marriage of "Trivia King" as I was always competitive in games, like Trivial

Pursuit, that we played with our friends. I enjoyed reading from a young age. (Remember, "Oh, Lloyd, you and your books"?) And of course, I loved reading about history – which is a study that includes millions of minute details.

During a class period one day, there was a knock at the door. A student from an English teacher's class had come to ask me an obscure question about the career of the daughter of Fidel Castro. I responded, "She had a radio program in Miami that attacked her father in Cuba." For the remainder of the day, students came to my class after that English class and said, "How did you know that?"

I include this here because it was always important for me to stay current on world events, knowledgeable on historical details and up to date on many other subjects, including good teaching strategies. Even though my history lessons were permanently burned into my mind to the point that notes were not even necessary for my teaching, I consistently added interesting facts that I would learn from my own reading habits.

Control Your Anger On and Off the Field

Although I enjoyed teaching a great deal, I also loved my time as a high school football coach. Because I had been a football defensive lineman when I was in high school, I had had many examples of both good and bad coaches.

When it was my turn to be an authority figure, I knew I must approach coaching the boys as I would approach teaching my students in class – with dignity and respect. I was not perfect and there were definitely moments when I slipped from being the role model I wanted to be. But for the most part, I tried not to yell and cuss at the players when we were on the field during practices or games. I got word one day that a player's mother made the statement that her son liked me better because I didn't cuss or scream like the other coaches.

The same behavior must be shown to all students. I believe a teacher will lose respect of the students (and in fact, with co-workers and supervisory staff) when he is unable to control his actions or his words. Students pay close attention to the examples that their teachers set in front of them. Always present the best you that you can!

***Always do your best. What you plant now,
you will harvest later.
~Og Mandino***

$$\boxed{\textbf{LESSONS LEARNED}}$$

BE THE BEST YOU CAN BE ... ALWAYS!

1.   As teachers, we get one chance at each student we educate. We are not in a business where we are able to recall our product and work on them again to fix them or make them better (like a car manufacturer). There are no "do-overs" or "recalls."

2.   Keep good notes on each lesson, unit or chapter that you teach and whether or not it was successful. Include changes you would make and refer to those the next time you present this material. Try implementing fresh approaches or different strategies to each lesson.

3.   Having detailed lesson plans, including high quality activities, projects and questioning strategies, keeps you on track during your class period. Make every minute count!

4.   Go into every workshop and in-service opportunity with a positive attitude and vow to learn at least one new strategy or method to implement into your lessons.

7

STRATEGY SEVEN

Parents are People Too

*Any fool can be happy...It takes a man with a real heart to
make beauty out of the stuff that makes you weep.
Clive Barkeer, Days of Magic, Nights of War*

*Each day of our lives we make deposits in the memory
banks of our children.
~Charles R. Swindoll*

*It is easier to build strong children than to repair broken
men.
~Frederick Douglass*

Calls to Parents

If there is a task that teachers dread most, it might be
calling parents. The reason for this reluctance could be the

responses teachers sometimes receive from parents. Reactions can range from "my child thinks you don't like him" to "she just doesn't like your subject." I once had a parent tell me that she could not do anything with him at home. "So what makes you think I can make him do anything for you at school. That is your job!"

One day word came down from central office that teachers were expected to call every parent of students who were struggling with their grades. So, at the end of the day, I gathered my grade book and retreated to the phone. The first call I made was to the home of Robert. He seemed to struggle with paying attention and remaining fully awake at all times. His grandmother answered the phone and after I identified myself and shared my concern for Robert's situation, his grandmother was immediately thankful for the call. She explained that she was 83 years old and that she and Robert survived on her Social Security. To help with the costs of living, Robert had taken a job after school that started at 4:00. He worked until midnight and it was often 1:00 AM before he got home. I shared with his grandmother that she or Robert should let me know when circumstances were overwhelming him and that I would work with him as much as I could.

My second call was to the home of Linda who was struggling to finish homework. Her mother explained that her husband had lost his job in the economic downturn and, as a result, they had lost their home and for some time they hadn't known where they would be sleeping on any night. She opened up to me by saying that they had stayed with friends, at motels and in their car. As a consequence of all this uncertainty, the family had not focused on what was happening at school. I was speechless and found it difficult to find the right words.

My final call that day was to the family of Juan who seemed to have completely lost the ability to focus. The father told me that he had recently been diagnosed with stage four cancer. He told me that his doctor had advised that the family should get their affairs in order. Once again, their son's lack of attention to school had gotten lost in the shuffle and the life-changing diagnosis.

After these three calls, I found myself mentally exhausted. Over the next few days, I began to look at these students through a different perspective. I realized that these students and parents were dealing with some of life's most difficult decisions and situations and doing their best under the circumstances.

A Matter of Life and Death

Teachers must develop positive working relationships with the parents as well as the students. One example of this brings to mind a serious situation to which I was sort of a bystander witness. A senior staff member, I'll refer to him as Mr. Phillips, discovered that a student had written a mild obscenity about him on a desktop in his classroom. The next day Mr. Phillips threatened an entire class with reprisals if the guilty person did not confess. When no one confessed, in a fit of anger, he disassembled all of the desks and piled all of the desktops in the corner of the room.

That day the students were forced to attempt to do their written work or tests on their laps. One student complained to his parent that they were being forced to do their written work without the benefit of a writing surface. This parent called the school and spoke with Mr. Phillips. The conversation grew heated. The parent scheduled an appointment for the following morning during the teacher's conference period to have a face-to-face discussion.

The school had a small conference room off of the main office that was regularly used as a coffee room for early-arriving teachers. On that particular morning, I arrived at the school earlier than usual. While checking my mailbox, I took a seat in the coffee room with a close friend. After a few minutes of light conversation, Mr. Phillips arrived as well, carrying a large collegiate-style dictionary. He was muttering and cursing under his breath. My friend, taking note of Mr. Phillips' agitated state, asked what was wrong. In response, Mr. Phillips explained that he had a parent conference scheduled and planned on shooting the parent. (Of course, he called him worse things than parent.)

He then sat the dictionary on the table and opened it, revealing a gun. My friend and I exchanged a look of disbelief and became alarmed. He proceeded to tell us how he had spent the night carefully using an X-acto knife to carve out the cavity in the book to hold the gun. My friend immediately left the room and found the administrator on duty and reported this exchange, explaining that the parent conference that was about to take place could not be held. We never learned what action was taken, but needless to say, Mr. Phillips never returned to school! To this day, it still amazes me that such a minor incident can fester into a potential fatal situation.

Open House

Open House, or parent night at the high school, should be acknowledged as a very important event. I always seemed to have a good turnout of parents on this night. (I wanted to think that it was because they really wanted to meet me; but it was because I had AP students, whose parents always seem to be more involved.) For whatever reason they were there, I was grateful. Since there is only a short amount of time with each group, this time should be well planned. Getting the pertinent information from each of them (especially various methods of communication) is critical. Share the most important things about your class and the way that you run your class so that parents can grasp your expectations.

I always shared with the parents at Open House that it was my policy to return phone calls, texts, emails, etc. before leaving school everyday. I wanted the parents to know that their calls were important. As a parent myself, I was frustrated when I did not receive a prompt reply from one of my children's teachers.

A common comment from parents is "If I'd only known about this." Establishing a system or method of publicizing projects, test dates, important due dates, make-up policies, retesting guidelines and the course syllabus will keep parents informed. Put yourself in their place and consider what you would want provided.

PARENTS ARE PEOPLE TOO

1.   The Internet provides multiple methods to keep parents informed as to what your expectations and class rules are and what projects and deadlines are coming up. This can also include tutorial schedule, conference periods, extra credit opportunities and more.

2.   Use any method you can to keep the lines of communication open to help eliminate the unexpected.

3.   By eliminating the "I didn't know that factor," you can greatly reduce the number of angry phone calls to the school administration that keeps everybody happy.

8

STRATEGY EIGHT

Stand on Your Principles

That you may retain your self respect. It is better to displease the people by doing what you know is right, than to temporarily please them by doing what you know is wrong, so that you may be able to better discover with accuracy the peculiar bent of the genius of each.
~Plato

Productivity is never an accident. It is always the result of a commitment to excellence, intelligent planning and focused effort.
~ Paul J. Meyer

Make Your Policies Clear

At one particular point in my career, there was a great deal of concern nationally regarding the growing trend of cheating in both public schools and in college. After a great deal of consideration, I decided to adopt a strategy that I hoped would address any problem I failed to recognize. On each of my unit tests, I always included an essay question because I believed it was essential that my students knew how to compose a scholarly essay. To this end, at the beginning of a unit, I would make my students aware of three possible questions that might be selected for the test. As they studied the material for the unit, they were instructed to gather information to be prepared to answer the essay selected for the exam. Essay prep notes were not allowed on the exam.

Unfortunately, in spite of my best intentions, I caught a young lady with a prepared "cheat sheet" for each of the essay questions. At the start of that year, I put into place a new policy for my classes. If a student was completely unprepared for a unit test, he or she could petition me for a chance to take another version of the exam at a time of my choosing. This included the provision that the student must explain why they were unprepared. I did this in attempt to prevent students from repeatedly "blowing off" test preparation. Additionally, I informed both students and parents that if a student chose to cheat on an exam despite the opportunity to postpone the test, the offender would receive no points on the test and an "unsatisfactory" conduct grade for the grading period.

While I monitored my classes during an exam about halfway through the school year, I noticed a student behaving strangely during the test. As I continued to observe, I realized that the student had concealed a cheat sheet under her paper to help her write a good essay. When confronted, the student was remorseful. As was my custom, I required her to write an explanation of what she had done. Her greatest concern seemed to be that she would be ineligible for an extracurricular competition the following week. I found out later that her father, who was furious at the punishment, stormed into the front office after school demanding that his daughter should not have to suffer the consequences of her actions.

The following morning, I was summoned to the principal's office. When I arrived, I found a semicircle of chairs and vice principals surrounding the solitary chair in which I was directed to sit. I felt that I was about to undergo an inquisition. Immediately, one of the assistants demanded that I rescind the punishment. When I refused to consider it, the principal asked why I would not simply let this go. I explained that there were 150 other students in my classes who were sure an exception would be made for this student. Then I explained my policy in which I give all students another option rather than dishonesty. After a few minutes, he indicated that he felt the punishment was justifiable.

I soon had a second conference with this parent who displayed greater anger at the consequences than the action of his daughter that brought on the consequences. When pressed, I explained that dishonesty merited my actions. In spite of reading the confession of cheating by his daughter and having her admit to her actions in the conference, he insisted she was merely trying to gain a "competitive edge."

In many ways, education is similar to other professions in that there will always be those who will try to persuade you that ethics, morality and principles are not worth the effort. I would urge all who enter education to establish a clear set of professional values and hang on to them for dear life. Even if you do not realize it, your students are watching and learning this lesson that goes far beyond academics.

Standing Firm for Traditions

Each year at the conclusion of the school year, it was tradition for the entire school to gather together in an assembly to honor achievement by outstanding seniors. Each department in the school selected a senior who had exhibited outstanding scholarship for the four years they attended our school. I would gather the entire history department to discuss possible honorees for history. Inevitably, more than one department chose students for an award. In order to recognize as many students as possible, the faculty developed a position of asking a student who was nominated for more than one award, which award he/she would prefer to receive. Our thinking was that since it was the student's award, they should be given the choice of which award they preferred because they might be applying for particular programs in college in which an award in the chosen field might enhance the resume. This process was always monitored by one of the school's administrators.

One year, the administrator overseeing the process was new to our school, having been removed from a previous position for administrative policy abuse. As usual, a student was nominated for more than one award, and the administrator in question announced to the group that it would be her decision as to who would receive the award. I quickly stepped forward and explained to her that we had a longstanding position in such a case of allowing the student to decide which award he or she preferred. The administrator announced that tradition or not she would make the decision even though being new to the school she had very little first hand knowledge of the students and their academic accomplishments that would merit their being honored. I was not only discouraged but frankly angered as well at this administrator's authoritarian attitude toward what had traditionally been a cooperative and successful process. I was informed that regardless of past practices the administrator was going to make these decisions. I indicated that no decision was going to be final until the principal had been allowed the opportunity to weigh in on the situation. I was then told that I would not be allowed to speak to the principal without this administrator's permission. My response to this threat was to tell the administrator that she could watch me walk out of the door to the principal's office. When I explained the dilemma to the principal, the reply was that we would follow the longstanding tradition to give the student the opportunity to choose the award. In the midst of this explanation, the assistant principal arrived in the principal's office only to learn that her impetuous and ill-conceived decision had been overruled.

Incidents such as this can serve only to discourage teachers from acting in the best interests of the students and disillusionment with our profession. For those of you who find yourself in a similar situation where your ethics and core beliefs are being challenged, I would recommend a careful reading of my wife's book, *To Love to Teach Again: 10 Secrets to Rekindling Passion to Keep You in the Classroom* (Amazon.com).

"Great spirits have always encountered violent opposition"
~Albert Einstein

"Good Trouble"

The longer a teacher stays in the classroom the greater the possibility that they will run into opposition to how and what they teach. For me, that moment came in the midpoint of my career and from the most unexpected direction, the Ku Klux Klan and other like-minded individuals.

One spring I received a note from central administration concerning a visit from a reporter from the largest newspaper in the state. When I spoke to the reporter, he explained that he was doing a story on how various schools and teachers were dealing with the upcoming black history month.

I explained that I did not devote only a single month to black history, women's history, Native American history or any other important group in American history. I felt that devoting only a single month to each of these groups was demeaning to their contributions. Instead I emphasized their contributions in each and every period that we covered in the class. We agreed to a date for him to spend a day observing my classes.

The visit was supposed to take only one day of classes but at the end of the day he asked if he could return the next day for further observation. I agreed, and he returned not only the following day but also the three days left in the week.

I fully expected the story to be a small one relegated to the back of the paper or buried in the less significant sections. So I was greatly surprised when on the expected date of publication, the story appeared on the front page detailing my very different approach to teaching black history.

I was late arriving home from school that afternoon and arrived to find that my answering machine was completely full of messages. As I checked the messages, I was shocked to find that there were many vulgar, thinly veiled threats regarding my emphasis on black history. That night my phone rang again and when I answered it, I was met by a torrent of abusive language. When I was finally able to get a word in the caller asked me what African American had ever accomplished other than sports and dancing. (The word he used was not African American, but I choose not to write it here.)

This was the wrong thing to ask someone who was well versed in black history. I immediately began to list the accomplishments of prominent black Americans and figures in World History. The more I named, the angrier and more abusive the caller became. I finally ended the call when the obscenities and racial slurs became too much to tolerate. The caller ended the conversation with an indirect warning that I might become the target of groups that would not approve of my attitude toward the teaching of black history. The following day I reported the incident to my supervisor and the local police were asked to keep a closer eye on suspicious individuals hanging around the school.

The bizarre nature of this incident continued for several weeks as I continued to receive angry and vaguely threatening calls. Gradually the phone calls tapered off and were replaced with unsolicited letters containing every type of racist rhetoric imaginable.

While a teacher may encounter opposition from outside the school, they may also face roadblocks erected by those within the system. When children enter a school system at the kindergarten or first grade level they are sometimes encouraged to always stay within the lines at all times. Teachers who may stray from the rigid lines of district curriculum can become the target of internal criticism. One such instance would be the years I chose to supplement the instruction of American history by utilizing E. D. Hirsch's widely acclaimed book, *Cultural Literacy: What Every American Should Know*. Over the next six years an untold number of students remarked how much they had enjoyed the book and had continued to use it in their college studies. One administrator from the central office made it a point to make critical remarks concerning the book.

Even though I have never put a great deal of emphasis on standardized test scores, during the time frame that I used Dr. Hirsch's book I only had one student in those six years who failed to pass the state exam. This meant that one student out of around 360 students passed the exam and a number of students remarked that many of the questions answers came from knowledge gained from the use of the very book that a member of the central office who seldom entered a working classroom criticized without actual information about Dr. Hirsch's book.

Teachers must choose to do what is best for their students, not mindlessly. Just as children should be encouraged to think outside the box, teachers should be allowed to plan outside the lines.

STAND ON YOUR PRINCIPES

1.   Establish your policies and make them clear to the students and their parents.

2.   Hold on to certain chosen principles because our students are being raised in a generation of situational ethics. I found that one of the most important lessons that I could impart to my students was to stand up for what they believed in.

3.   Be diligent in the job that you are doing. When you challenge the norm, it gives you the ability to stand on your own two feel to face the opposition.

4. Cling to your beliefs.

9

STRATEGY NINE

Spare the Rod

Do not train a child to learn by force or harshness; but direct them to it by what amuses their minds, so that you may be better able to discover with accuracy the peculiar bent of the genius of each.
Plato

Set High Expectations

One incident always comes to mind when I consider the benefits of a proper perspective on classroom discipline. One day my principal asked me to represent the school on a district committee that was to consider changes to the district policies. I would miss a day of school to attend so I had arranged for a substitute to cover my classes. I carefully spelled out the lesson plans, instructions and class rolls for each period.

The day after the district meeting I was delighted to return to my classroom to find the student assignments neatly stacked by class periods on my desk – and in alphabetical order! Additionally, a list of absent students was included in each collection.

As my first class began, I casually remarked to the class that things must have gone well with the substitute. Imagine my shock when several students spoke up to tell me that there had been no substitute. I asked each succeeding class and heard the same answer. I asked, "Who checked the roll, handed out the assignments and had gone over the directions?" Two young men in that first class were quickly identified as having taken charge of the class. "When no substitute arrived to supervise the class," they explained, "we took it upon ourselves to do what we knew you would want." They checked the roll, passed out papers and went over the directions that I had written. At the end of class, they collected all of the work and lingered behind as students arrived for the next class. Selecting a trustworthy student, they passed on instructions and suggested that she do the same for the next class. This was done throughout the day.

While I was so grateful for their help and proud of the way these students took charge, I was quite upset that my classes were left unsupervised for the entire day. When I had an opportunity, I went to the front office to visit with the person in charge of subs. When I questioned her about the substitute that I had arranged, she shared that an administrator decided that the sub was needed elsewhere in the building without making arrangements for other adults to cover my classes.

While I knew that I was not at fault, I was concerned that there would not have been someone in charge had there been an incident during class. When I confronted the administrator who made this decision, he seemed unconcerned. He stated that he had stopped by my classroom several times during the day to check on the students. "Each time I stopped by your class, the students were working quietly," he claimed. My response was, "Did you not notice that there was no adult in the room?"

The students behaved the way they did because I believed that there had been a clear set of expectations. I had also spent a lot of time establishing good relationships with the students, which included building trust. I believe that had I acted as a tyrant during the year, I would not have seen this kind of responsible behavior. Many teachers constantly admonish students (high school in particular) to "grow up and behave as adults," yet too often students are not given the opportunity to demonstrate that they can behave as adults. I still marvel at the thought of dozens of seventeen-year-old students behaving well and completing their assignments while being completely unsupervised.

Sometimes Bending the Rules is Best

During one of the many summer school sessions in which I taught, I had a student named Terri who had attended my school the year before. Because I knew of her, I remembered that she had dealt with a somewhat difficult home life. She began to miss classes and the principal threatened to remove her from summer school, which would have denied her the opportunity to receive the necessary credits she needed to advance.

I approached the principal and pled Terri's case. I asked that she would be allowed to continue to stay in school. The summer school principal, with whom I had not worked previously, later expressed that she was surprised that a teacher would advocate for a student to remain in class. I kept Terri in class for the rest of the semester. I reminded her daily, "You need to be here tomorrow."

Students Respect Those Who Discipline Them

Thirteen straight years passed during my thirty-five in the classroom before I ever sent a student to the office for disciplinary reasons. I did not want to give the students the impression that there was any classroom situation with which I was incapable of dealing. Additionally, I refused to cede control of disciplinary situations to an administrator with little or no knowledge of the student. Instead, I chose to deal with these situations one on one with a student in order to reach a mutually amicable resolution. My only exception to this policy was in the case of a student cheating on an exam. I would submit an incident report to the appropriate administrator marked "For notifications only – no further action required." As I have detailed, I always allowed for a student to take advantage of alternative testing options rather than cheat on an exam, jeopardizing other eligibilities for elected positions within the student hierarchy (i.e., student council, cheerleader, club officer, etc.). In dealing with these situations, which was rare, I required that the student in question provide me with a written confession of their actions and motivations. This seemed to be painful enough punishment for most students.

As my wife, as an administrator, always reminded her teachers, the person who deals with the discipline of a student the most, has the most influence over that student.

121

If the assistant principal is always the one to counsel the student and to assign any punishment, then the teacher loses respect and the relationship that the teacher desires and should require.

That this policy was successful was demonstrated to me on one occasion when a student had rather obviously been caught in the act of dishonesty by me. Later, another student shared with me that they would never do this because they wouldn't want to disappoint me.

LESSONS LEARNED

SPARE THE ROD

1.   Be judicious in your discipline. Ration it like you would food in a pandemic. Repeated attempts at disciplining for niggling reasons results in a decline in classroom discipline.

2. Constant threats of disciplinary action can lead to the exact opposite of the desired goal of effective classroom management.

3. In building positive teacher-student relationships, discipline and/or encouragement are most successful when carried out in a one-to-one circumstance.

4.   While some student behavior certainly calls for disciplinary action, the effective teacher recognizes the difference between trivial and significant misbehavior. For an example, a discipline referral for not having a pencil is a trivial behavior and you, the teacher, should deal with this problem with an appropriate punishment.

10

STRATEGY TEN

Keep the Faith

*Don't worry that children never listen to you; worry that
they are always watching you.*
~*Robert Fulghum*

Grateful

On the day of my retirement, I chose to skip the end of
school faculty luncheon and slipped out of the school
unnoticed, knowing that the principal would be glad to see
me gone. Much to my surprise as I locked my door for the
last time, I was greeted by a couple of hundred of students
and some of their children all holding signs wishing me
well. While I am not given to outward displays of
emotion, I could not help but reflect on the fact that mine

125

had indeed been a life well lived. Once again, my deep thanks to the six to seven thousand students with whom I crossed paths. I hope I may have impacted your life. You impacted my life many times over.

Hopeful

In the era of Covid-19, we have seen the creation of what I would call "social and economic orphans." Studies have shown a growing rate of depression among our children and we have yet to determine the long-term impact on student learning from this pandemic. Children are being placed in front of televisions as a substitute for babysitting and human interaction. I do not believe that parents are deliberately abandoning their children, but are forced to in order to find gainful employment to provide for them. As a result of all of this, the role of the teacher is not only a disperser of knowledge but will become even more important in the post-pandemic era as an emotional support. Because of what we are currently experiencing due to the 2020-2021 pandemic, there is a critical need for teachers to remain dedicated to providing quality education for our young people.

**The tiny seed knew that in order to grow,
it would need to be dropped in the dirt, covered in
darkness, and would struggle to reach the light.
~Unknown**

Humbled

Teachable moments don't have to happen in the classroom; they come along when you least expect them. Shortly after I retired in 2012, I suffered two severe strokes just two months later, as I have already referenced. I was left with an inability to walk or speak well. After my release from 10 weeks of hospitalization from three hospitals, including five weeks in Baylor Rehabilitation Hospital in Dallas, I began what was to be a nine-month regimen of daily therapy. This was five days a week from 8:00 to 5:00 everyday. My speech therapist gave me a series of exercises to do to restore strength in my vocal cords, which had been damaged by one of the strokes. Part of this therapy, I was required to practice a series of strenuous vocal exercises that sounded very much like a flock of distressed geese.

As these exercises were somewhat embarrassing to perform around others, I would retreat to the patio of the therapy center to go through my drills. I soon found that I was not the only client who needed to perform these vocal exercises on a daily basis. A young man, named William, had suffered a similar injury due to encountering gang violence in his neighborhood. Day after day, William and I would sequester ourselves from the rest of the group, which I suppose would have been humorous had I not been involved. He and I would talk about his life in a violent gang-dominated environment, something that I was completely unfamiliar with.

As our therapy progressed, William became fascinated with my practice of always bringing a book with me everyday, which I would read in brief moments between therapy sessions. One day he asked me where I got all of those books. I explained that for many years my family's go-to present for Christmas and birthdays was a gift card for local bookstores. I still remember William somewhat wistfully telling me that no one had ever bought him a book.

Knowing that his birthday was coming up, I went home that day and asked my wife to purchase William a book and a book store gift card that I could give to him on his birthday. He seemed amazed at this gift and expressed confusion as to what kind of book he should buy. William imitated my habit of reading at the center when he had an opportunity. I missed several days of therapy due to illness. When I returned, I found that he had been released from therapy. I lost touch with William and have never known if he continued reading. Regardless of whether he continued to pick up a book, I still found a degree of satisfaction knowing that I had made an impression on William to continue reading and learning.

128

Committed

As this book comes to its close, I offer some final simple and effective strategies for building teacher-student relationships.

- Put your heart into your lesson plans. Focus just as much on getting to know and guiding yours students as you do on teaching academic concepts.
- At the beginning of the year or semester, discuss your and your students' expectations as a class. Hold individual meetings to help struggling students reach their goals.
- Learn how to construct positive comments by giving, specific compliments (e.g. 'you're not as bad as you used to be').
- Make sure you keep healthy boundaries with your students. If a student upsets or frustrates you, don't take it personally or bring it home with you.
- Model a positive atmosphere for students.
- Make a personal contact with each student as he or she enters class.
- Create a welcoming and learning atmosphere by decorating your classroom with subject-related displays. Include student-created projects.

- At the start of each day and somewhere in your class, outline or summarize on a board in the class the learning expectations for the day.
- At the start of each semester, clearly define expectations for student learning, i.e. the ability to write a college-level essay by the end of the year.
- On a regular basis, place students with a classmate or a small group to encourage mastery of working with a team.

Wishing You Well

I wish for you, as a new or veteran teacher, positive relationship-building with your own students. This was always a priority in my entire teaching career; therefore, I look back on those thirty-five years with great satisfaction and pride. May your career be the same for you!

LESSONS LEARNED

KEEP THE FAITH

1. Recognize and acknowledge when you have good administrative leadership. Build good relationships with them. Be grateful for having leaders who are just as committed to your students as you are.

2. With the guidance of dedicated teachers who strive to provide excellent instruction, I am hopeful that our next generation will be made of thoughtful citizens and leaders of integrity. Hopefully, our country, the United States of America, will elevate the role of educators to the same standing of esteem and respect that other industrialized nations do.

3. I have been appreciative and humbled by the honors that I have received during my career. But I would be amiss if I did not give credit to those who supported me since my own time as a student in a classroom. Great teachers, inspiring school leaders and dedicated students made my pathway to success possible.

EPILOGUE

The Words of Others

Children must be taught how to think, not what to think.
Margaret Mead

People's blessings give you the power to work tirelessly.
The only thing required is commitment.
~Narendra Modi

Social media has allowed me through the years since my stroke to keep in touch with students from years past – some are even from the distant past. I've posed questions, had conversations, shared some opinions and have offered congratulations and condolences to many of them. While writing this book, I reached out to former students for comments and suggestions on my teaching methodologies, classroom procedures and anything else they wanted to share.

My sincerest thanks to all of you whose messages are included in this book! *I continue to welcome other comments at any time that could be included in my next work!*

"You didn't teach me how to think. You taught me to teach myself to think: how to take facts and organize them, how to compare facts to theories … and the difference between the two … and how to question yourself and when my 'truth' didn't match-up with the real truth. You taught me to swallow hard and accept the real truth even if it hurts. I also used the note-taking system you taught us all the way through college and my architectural-licensure exams. My wife learned a similar way of taking notes and between us, we have passed them on to our son."
~William Hodge

"I sat in your class on 9/11. Ten years to that day I was in Afghanistan on the first of my three deployments. I believe my desire to serve in the military and my love for history was cemented in your classroom and I doubt I would have lived the life I have without you."
~Gregory Scroadie Harris

"I watched in tears as the second tower fell in that class too! Now I proudly build the wiring harnesses that get installed in military aircraft. You taught me to do my own research, form my own opinions and be strong in my beliefs. I vote every chance I get because you taught me how important my voice can be."
~Stacey Marissa Zenteno

"For me, Mr. Sizemore, you showed me how adults should be. You were such a great person and smart and funny and strict but not too strict. You were an adult in my life as a teenager that I could look up to and aspire to be like. It seems so small. It is not as if you ever did anything specifically, for me, per se. But you were just yourself and you were such a smart, stable, cool, smart person that I just looked up to you so much. That's really it; I looked up to you. I felt safe and on the right path in your class. I want you to know what a difference it made in my life (and my big sister's life too) to have been your student."
~Sonya Worden-Eudaly

"Not only did you change my heart for history, we all lived it in 2001, and watched it unfold since. I still believe in history as a part of our past and without extraordinary educators such as you, history will keep repeating itself. Education is a bridge for a brighter future. Though I did not choose education as my profession I am honored to care for people and learn to love each one as a part of my family, including you and Mrs. Sizemore. I am still blessed to have you guys in my life."
~Sherry Escobar

"While I am certainly not a history buff, my time in your class was spent truly engaging in historical facts and I

thank you for that. If we don't learn about our history, we are destined to repeat it and that is not all good things."
~Shanna Toft

"I owe quite a bit of my success in life, to you, Mr. Sizemore. You and your teaching got me through university and law school. I still think about you and what you would think of me. I always wanted to make you proud. You remind me of my favorite professor at the University of Texas, George Forgie. Superior intellects both."
~Lisa Roemmich

"Even though you are a man, you made school feel like a true 'alma mater' which is Latin for 'nurturing mother.' This is my philosophy now that I am a teacher. What do I teach? Latin! How did I learn Latin? I taught myself! I have taught Latin for 16 years and my love of teaching grows more each year. Mr. Sizemore, I count you among my best teachers."
~Lara Sowell

"History was never really my thing, but you made your class interesting and I always looked forward to your period. One thing that sticks in my mind was that you made us memorize our driver's license and Social Security

numbers. To this day I have them memorized. I became a teacher in a rural south Texas school district and I am completing my 28th year. This district is located in an area where there is so much history you learn about in school."
~Kari Williams Deforest

"You benched me in the 2nd half of a varsity soccer game because I decided to try my hand at coaching. I learned my lesson because I wanted to play. You later coached me as a kicker and member of the special teams in football."
~Terry Ambrose

"Funny thing – I never actually had you for a class but your passion and expectations of student performance was so well known amongst my peers, I 'feel' like I did have you."
~James Earp

"First thing that comes to my mind is [that] …I am for one so grateful that I was given the opportunity to be taught by you. Although you've had a number of students, it also saddens me that there are a great deal more that will miss that opportunity…. You were by far my favorite history teacher and … after your class I was more intrigued in history than ever. …You made me love history so much that I wanted to teach it and learn more about it. It was because of your passion to teach history that gave me that

137

small spark that history is interesting and we can learn a lot from it. …You not only made an impact on my life but to other students as well. Your class notes, lectures, quizzes, and tests helped me prepare for college. You're a remarkable teacher that will never be forgotten and I hope that when I become a teacher I'm just as great as you. Our school will definitely not be the same without you."
~Cecilia Rodriguez, Class of 2009

"You were one of my favorite teachers ever. …Your class was full of so many fun times and you made history, which is already something I love, even more fun, and I didn't think that was even possible. You're just so kind and amazing and I [will} miss being able to go to your class everyday. I've told people multiple times that you're such a great teacher and that you show people what a good teacher should be like. You're kind, you listen to your students, you help them, and I never saw you get angry and yell at the class. … You're one of those teachers who inspires others and can make them feel good about themselves; I really respect you. …It's all good memories. I think that people who didn't have you as a teacher missed out on something amazing, and I feel lucky that I got to experience having you as my teacher. "
~Wednesday Little

"Congratulations on being such an amazing teacher…. You made History fun. I always loved hearing fun facts about historical figures and events. (Wilmer McLean had the Civil War start on his front lawn and end in his front parlor. Benjamin Franklin was a ladies man.) You have such an immense source of knowledge that you love sharing with your students. It was amazing how compassionate you were about your job and that really helped many students. Thank you for sharing your knowledge, enthusiasm and your support."
~Megan Hodges

Thanks for Teaching Us

Your smile when you spoke…
It made me smile
Your touch was what helped me each day
The love in your voice made me love you
And now it's my turn to say…
Thanks for teaching us.

The wink in your eye made me happy
The note that you wrote made me glad
The hug that you gave showed you loved me
How'd you know that I was feeling sad?

I look into your eyes and see reflections of
Not what I am right now – but what I can become

Thank you for showing me kindness
Thank you for teaching with love
Thank you for being here
When you could be anywhere
Thank you – thank you – thank you!

Author Unknown

www.ingramcontent.com/pod-product-compliance
Lightning Source LLC
Chambersburg PA
CBHW052033150726
48002CB00002B/587